Bishop T. D. Jakes

Help Me To Fit in My Own Church

ALBURY PUBLISHING
Tulsa, Oklahoma

Scripture quotations marked KJV are taken from *The King James Version* of the Bible.

Scripture quotations marked NAS are taken from the *New American Standard Bible*. Copyright © The Lockman Foundation 1960, 1962, 1963, 1968, 1971, 1972, 1973, 1975, 1977. Used by permission.

Help Me Fit in My Own Church
ISBN 1-57778-197-X
Copyright © 1997, 2000 by T. D. Jakes
T. D. Jakes Ministries
International Communications Center
P. O. Box 210887
Dallas, Texas 75211

Published by ALBURY PUBLISHING
P. O. Box 470406
Tulsa, Oklahoma 74147-0406

Printed in the United States of America.
All rights reserved under International Copyright Law.
Contents and/or cover may not be reproduced in whole or part in any form without written consent of the Publisher.

I think that this is a subject that needs desperately to be discussed. It is often difficult for many people to develop the ability to catch the vision of the local church and flow into an arena that causes them to feel a part of that vision. There are many contributing factors that make this challenging.

Generally people with aggressive or assertive behaviors struggle to submit to a pre-existing vision. They have a tendency to want to come in and alter the vision. This is often done without malice. It is veiled in a sincere desire to help.

The problem lies in the fact that their skills are often good, but many times they have not learned the wisdom of flowing with the current vision that already exists. Instead they plunge headlong into areas and ideas without learning how to mesh with the vision that exists.

These assertive, highly aggressive people are accustomed to being in control, and their first assignment is to learn to be a follower. It is important that they learn how to follow. It is that ability that helps them to become a good leader in the church.

I know that you may have been highly successful in the secular arena, but the requirements are different in the church. You must be under authority as well as in authority.

> *For I am a man under authority, having soldiers under me: and I say to this man, "go," and He goeth;*

and to another, "come," and He cometh; and to my servant, "do this," and He doeth it. When Jesus heard it, He marveled, and said to them that followed, "Verily, I say unto you, I have not found so great faith, no, not in Israel (Matthew 8:9-10 KJV).

Strangely enough, the man who said these words wasn't a religious man. He was actually a man who was a soldier. He wasn't an experienced Christian, but He understood authority.

If you understand authority, it will help you to flow into the mainstream of ministry without seeming abrasive to others. While you are learning the many differences that exist in how you might function and how the church with which you are associated functions, it will help you to remember that God called you to it and not it to you. You are there to learn. As long as they are teaching you truth according to Scripture, be a good student.

Getting In Order

Complying with the vision is not optional; it is a necessity. It is only when we have order that we experience the corporate blessing that God wants the church as a whole to enjoy.

Have you ever seen a two-headed animal? If you did, it was an accident of nature. Generally, there are not any around. Likewise, you must know that it is God's will that there be leadership and order. You are called to flow with that order. "Remember those who led you, who spoke the Word of God to you; and considering the result of their conduct, imitate their faith." (Hebrews 13:7 NAS)

I often study text by examining key words. The key words in this text are: "remember," "consider," and "imitate". What are we to remember? We are to remember those who are in leadership. That means that we are instructed not to move without being mindful and submitted to those who are designated by God to lead.

It is God who gives them authority, and we are instructed to comply. That doesn't mean that they are perfect or that they are always correct. They may have made a business decision or an appointment that you feel was unwise. It may be a personal nuance of theirs. It may even be that they exercise poor judgment in dealing with people or even unfortunately deal unfairly with you. You still must realize that these are the ones God chose as leaders. They will grow in their leadership abilities. Sometimes the road looks a lot different from the back seat than it does from the front.

The Bible says to consider their lifestyle. If what they are teaching doesn't appear fruitful for them, then it might be cause for concern. We are not to choose our leaders by their popularity or charisma, but there should be a certain fruitfulness in their lives. It may not always be financial. It might be in terms of their consecration or commitment. Their love and faith in Christ Jesus may be the area that you want to emulate.

But there should be something in them that you would like to see duplicated in your own life. Consider the results of their conduct, their lifestyle.

Your pastor should have some positive results from his or her conduct. They might start out struggling, but eventually there should be some fruit.

Remember that neither fruit tree nor people are designed to produce fruit in their infancy. But certainly after maturity there ought to be some signs of fruition. If your spiritual leader has been walking in the Spirit effectively for years, you must consider that and appreciate anyone who maintains his/her commitment in this changing world.

The third thing that is significant is the word "imitate". We are advised to imitate their faith. I have often seen people imitate their leader's words, intonations, and body language. Some try to dress like their leaders or think like them. But what we are challenged to do is to imitate their faith.

You should be ready to experience an impartation of the anointing and the faith of your pastor in your own life. Their confidence in God should be contagious. You see, it would mean nothing to dress like a doctor, drive like a doctor, or write like one if you didn't know what he knew or thought what he thought.

Is Elisha In The House?

Understand that the greatest way you can move up in the Lord and flow with the vision is to serve. Serving not only creates humility, but it also assists you to find purpose in the house of the Lord. It is particularly a blessing for those who come into ministry and feel like they do not fit.

Get involved. Become a contributor of your time, your energies, your finances. When you serve, God gives you a special grace and anointing. It will never be attained through a tape or a book. It comes from yielding yourself to the work of the Lord.

Elisha was a young man who was destined to be great. But before he could reach his highest purpose of ministry, he was trained in serving the "set man." The set man was Elijah.

It was as Elisha served the man of God that he learned his own place and purpose in the kingdom. When all was said and done, Elisha ended up with more anointing and power than the man he served because he humbled himself. He literally received the faith and anointing of leadership by serving a man of God without creating division.

> *And Elijah said to Elisha, "Stay here, please, for the Lord has sent me as far as Bethel." But Elisha said, "As the Lord lives and as you yourself live, I will not leave you. So they went down to Bethel. Then the sons of the prophets who were at Bethel*

came out to Elisha and said to him, "Do you know that the Lord will take away your master from you today?" And he said, "Yes, I know; be still." And Elijah said to him, "Elisha, please stay here, for the Lord has sent me to Jericho.", but he said, "As the Lord lives, and as you yourself live, I will not leave you." So they came to Jericho(II Kings 2:2-4 NAS).

Now there were those who tried to dissuade him, but their efforts were not effective. Even Elijah himself could not persuade the prophet to flee his post. You see, Elisha's mind was set on serving where he was assigned.

You have been assigned to a particular ministry for a particular purpose. If you fail to get what God sent you there to receive, you will not be successful. The Bible said to imitate their faith! There are things that you will receive and things that you will give. If you never give what you have, you will never receive what you need. "Those that be planted in the house of the Lord shall flourish in the courts of our God. They shall bring forth fruit in old age; they shall be fat and flourishing" (Psalm 92:13-14 KJV).

Because Elisha stayed and bonded where he was assigned, a double portion of his mentor's anointing fell on him. He simply served his way into a great spiritual blessing. He was assigned there, and he served without distraction. He stayed so long that he had completely bonded with that ministry. He was eventually able to carry on the ministry that he had served under because he remained planted and allowed God to establish a bond in his life.

Harmony At All Cost

So the Word of God is challenging us to get the same mind set as our leaders so that we may be harmonious with the vision of the house.

God gives the vision to the "set man" who is the pastor. If you are sent to that ministry, you will want to adopt that same vision. If you do not, you will cause division. Division is the result of having two different visions. God never sends anyone to cause division. It is never God's will to cause dissension and discord. It would be better to leave quietly than to cause confusion and gender strife.

If you are involved or surrounded by anyone that seems to be causing division, you must immediately disassociate yourself from him or her. God will always judge a rebellious heart.

"But this people hath a revolting and a rebellious heart; they are revolted and gone. Neither say they in their heart, let us now fear the Lord our God, that giveth rain, both the former and the latter, in his season: He reserveth unto us the appointed weeks of the harvest. Your iniquities have turned away these things, and your sins have withholden good things from you. For among my people are found wicked men: they lay in wait, as he that setteth snares; they set a trap, they catch men" (Jeremiah 5:23-26 KJV).

Rebellion is the seventh abomination to the Lord. Abomination simply means that God despises it. I wouldn't want to be involved in anything that God despises. No wonder judgment falls behind it!! Rebellion carries a stench in the nostrils of God. If you have to apologize, do it. If you have to change your associates, do it. But whatever you do, do not allow the enemy to use you in this dangerous sin.

> *These six things doth the Lord hate: yea, seven are an abomination unto Him: a proud look, a lying tongue, and hands that shed innocent blood, an heart that deviseth wicked imaginations, feet that be swift in running to mischief, a false witness that speaketh lies, and he that soweth discord*

among the brethren (Proverbs 6:16-19 KJV).

Now a word about fitting in. If you do not allow God to cut the rough edges off of you, He cannot use you. It would be like a mason laying stones. Each stone is different in color, shape, and size. If the mason is going to use the stones, they often have to be cut. Do not think that God can set you in place without cutting some areas where your will is in the way of His purpose. He will have to be able to cut you in order to place you in the spot He has designed for you.

I am simply saying that you have to be willing to change. For some, that may mean holding your peace when you really want to react. For others, it may require learning timing and structure so that you go through the proper channels at the proper time to make your suggestions. If you are in love with your own opinion, you will be deeply pained because God will often cut and press you into tight situations where there may not be room for an opinionated person. There may not be room for sensitive feelings. He wants to use you, but working with others requires being cut to fit in the area that He has already been building.

No mason would tear down the whole wall to accommodate one stone. What he would do is cut the stone to accommodate the wall. Are you willing to be cut? You must be in the place that He has for you. When they were building Solomon's Temple, the Bible says that no hammers were heard. You see, when God gets ready to build, He cannot afford to have to cut you into place then. You have to be almost pre-cut. "and the house, when it was in building, was built of stone made ready before it was brought thither: so that there was neither hammer nor ax nor any tool of iron heard in the house, while it was in the building" (I Kings 6:7 KJV).

I have found that many things that I went through early in life helped to prepare me for His service. Notice the Word says that the "stone was made ready before it was brought hither". If you will look deep within yourself, God has been preparing you for change and flexibility. Do not allow anyone to waste that pre-cut experience that God used to prepare you for this place and time in your life. For what God wants to do in you, there will be no time for last minute hammers.

Fitting in with God is not generally the challenge. It is fitting in with the other stone that is a challenge. Our tendency is to want to change them; but have you ever considered that God may be using them to change you? Once you are in the position, it may be too late to go through the cutting. It is painful to have to learn your place while you are being used. It is like an actor having to learn their lines on stage.

You cannot accomplish God's will alone. You are going to have to learn how to flow with others. The ministry is not for super heroes but team players. It is when you learn the value of flowing with others, that God's highest purpose may be done in your life. It is the epitome of arrogance to assume that all others need to change to accommodate your mind set. True servants never even express an unsolicited opinion. Can you imagine going to a restaurant and the waitress comes to you and tells you what you should order? They do not because they are there to serve. Most people know nothing about serving, so they assume a servant's job without a servant's heart.

You see, the church was designed to be interdependent not independent. There really is no such thing as an independent church. No more than there is an independent member of your physical body. The members of your physical body are certainly not independent. They are interdependent.

You will learn as you serve that all of us have a function, and we should not criticize others for not being proficient in the area that we are efficient. You see, if my heart could breathe, who would pump blood?

But in fact God has arranged the parts in the body, every one of them, just as He wanted them to be. If they were all one part, where would the body be? As it is, there are any parts, but one body. The eye cannot say to the hand, "I don't need you!" And the head cannot say to the feet, "I don't need you!" (I Corinthians 12:18-21 NAS)

In closing, let me say this to you. You already fit a part and role that no other person can fit. If you will allow God to show you how to appreciate diversity, then you will not be frustrated in your place in the ministry. He doesn't want to use a hammer in the sanctuary. He wants to use His Word to bring you into alignment with a corporate vision. If you can submit, He can complete the job He has begun in your life. I know you may be uncomfortable from time to time. You may have to hold your peace and keep quiet when your opinion is swelling up inside. But remember He held His peace for you.

You have come to learn to work and to grow. So stop teaching a minute and realize that the greater class may be going on inside of you. The Master Himself may be teaching you something that if you will learn, it will cause multitudes to be saved. As you receive God's Word and will for your life, rest in the fact that He knows how to bring out the best in you.

If you have talents that are being overlooked, trust God that He, when He is finished working on the parts of you that are being perfected, will show all those around you what He has done when He is truly proud of how far you have come. Until then, make no stage for yourself, no murmuring or complaining. Just be still and know.

Know that when the time is right and the conditions are right, God will use you as a part of the team for His glory. Sometimes the test is to learn faith in God while He works on areas that we never even knew needed repair. When He is finished, He will set you in place. No one will ever even know that you were uncomfortable, and not a hammer will be heard because you will know how to fit into His will—even if His will cuts away at your flesh.

May I pray this simple prayer for you?

Lord, I know that I have much to offer, but I need you to teach me when and how to use what you have given me. As I am placed in this ministry, please do not allow me to miss the point and confuse the issue. I want to receive everything that I am supposed to receive. Give me the grace to work quietly without being recognized. Give me the strength to use times that I am not serving, to sharpen my tools, increase my faith, and develop my patience.

Heal me from my fears of rejection. Save me from the scars that I carry from past circumstances. I want to serve You, and I am willing to submit. I release You to cut away from my heart those rough edges that others may find offensive so that my personality will not get in the way of my purpose. Thank You, Lord, for using me at all. You could have chosen anyone. I am humbled to be asked to serve. Help me not to disappoint You with my old ways. In Jesus' name, I pray. Amen!

ABOUT THE AUTHOR
Bishop T. D. Jakes

T. D. Jakes is the founder and senior pastor of The Potter's House church in Dallas, Texas. A highly celebrated author with several bestselling books to his credit, he frequently ministers in massive crusades and conferences across the nation. His weekly television broadcast is viewed nationally in millions of homes.

Bishop Jakes resides in Dallas, Texas, with his wife Serita and five children.

To contact T. D. Jakes, write:

T. D. Jakes Ministries
International Communication Center
P. O. Box 210887
Dallas, Texas 75211

or visit his website at:

www.tdjakes.org

Books by T. D. Jakes

Six Pillars From Ephesians
(Series of six books)
Loved by God
Experiencing Jesus
Intimacy With God
Life Overflowing
Celebrating Marriage
Overcoming the Enemy
Woman, Thou Art Loosed! Devotional
Lay Aside the Weight
So You Call Yourself a Man?
*Devotions from Loose That Man &
Let Him Go!*
Woman, Thou Art Loosed!
Loose That Man & Let Him Go!
T. D. Jakes Speaks to Men!
T. D. Jakes Speaks to Women!

Videos by T. D. Jakes

*Six Pillars for the Believer: Insights of
Ephesians* Series (Six Videos)
The Rock for the Thirsty Soul
Overcoming Your Limitations
Praise in the Midst of Pain
Talk Your Way Out of It!
Don't Run From The Giant - Run To Him
Devil, I Want My Stuff

Also By T.D. Jakes

SINGLE CASSETTES/VIDEOS

Title	$6	$20
I Am Still In His Hands	☐	☐
The Kingdom Is Going To The Dogs	☐	☐
Your Faith Must Stand Trial	☐	☐
The Struggle Is Over	☐	☐
When The Dove Cries	☐	☐
Remember Lot's Wife	☐	☐
The Spell Is Broken	☐	☐
The Power of The Cross	☐	☐
Pass The Bread	☐	☐
Get Away From The Gate	☐	☐
If You Can Give It Up, You Can Have It All	☐	☐
Now!	☐	☐
Provoked	☐	☐
He Called Me Son	☐	☐
After This I Want My Stuff	☐	☐
The Blessed Man	☐	☐
Loose That Man And Let Him Go	☐	☐
The Price Of Power	☐	☐
Overcoming Silent Frustrations	☐	☐
Questions From The Cross	☐	☐
Chosen	☐	☐
The King Has A Crippled Child	☐	☐
Breaking The Spirit Of Failure	☐	☐
Leftovers	☐	☐
Naked And Not Ashamed	☐	☐
The Light Of The Word	☐	☐
Here Comes My Old Friend Again	☐	☐
Seeing What You Believe	☐	☐
This Is Not My Will To Be Like This	☐	☐
Rags To Riches	☐	☐

BOOKS/WORKBOOKS

Woman Thou Art Loosed	$9.95
Woman Thou Art Loosed/Wkbk.	$6.95
Can You Stand To Be Blessed?	$9.95
Can You Stand.../Wkbk.	$6.95
Water In The Wilderness	$6.95
Why?	$8.95
Why?/Notebook	$6.95
Naked And Not Ashamed	$11.95
Help, I've Fallen And Can't Get Up	$6.95
A Fresh Glimpse Of The Dove/Study Guide	$11.00
When Shepherds Bleed/Wkbk.	$10.00
Loose That Man And Let Him Go	$11.95
Loose That Man.../Wkbk.	$6.95
Harvest	$8.95
Harvest/Workbook	$6.95
Daddy Loves His Girls	$11.95

MINI-BOOKS

Lord, I Said I Wouldn't Fail You, But I Did!
Lord, I Miss My Time With You
Have You Received Since You Believed?
But, I Can't Afford To Tithe
Tithing Is A Matter Of Love...Not Law
Provoke God With Your Giving
I Choose To Forgive!
Saints With Sinner's Problems
Water Baptism: Who Needs It?
Help Me To Fit In My Own Church
Winning The Battle In Your Own Mind
It's Not Natural To Live Holy, It's Spiritual

A complete list of conferences, tapes, videos and books by T.D. Jakes is available by writing:
T.D. Jakes • P.O. Box 5390 • Dallas, TX 75208

Additional copies of this book and
other book titles
from ALBURY PUBLISHING are
available at your local bookstore.

ALBURY PUBLISHING
Tulsa, Oklahoma

For a complete list of our titles,
visit us at our website:
www.alburypublishing.com

For international and
Canadian orders,
please contact:

Access Sales International
2448 East 81st Street
Suite 4900
Tulsa, Oklahoma 74137
Phone 918-523-5590
Fax 918-496-2822